Lilies on the Moon

Poems by Robert W. Kurkela

Artwork by Cassidy S. Kurkela

Kidzpoetz Publishing
New City, New York

Lilies on the Moon

Second printing 2009

www.kidzpoetz.com

ISBN-13: 978-0-9760220-0-8   ISBN-10: 0-9760220-0-1

Library of Congress Control Number: 2004096251

Illustrations by Cassidy S. Kurkela

Book design by Janice M. Phelps
www.janicephelps.com

For my mom,
Lillian Saldon Kurkela

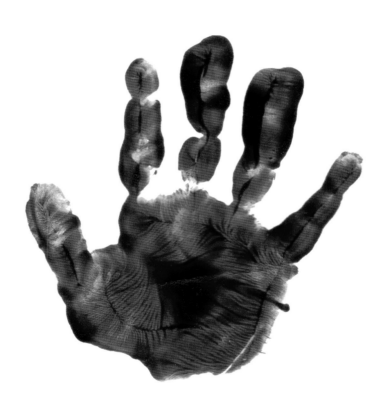

Words, Pranks And Charms

Oh how they giggle
When my words I form
For they never know
What I'll utter each morn.

Juice is what I want,
Yet apple won't do.
Grep is what I'll say
Grep is what I'll choose.

Cheerios...no dat!
Candy's what I crave.
Yet I have no choice,
Why should I behave?

I'll stir some trouble
And plunk from my milk.
Pretend it's otay,
Doggy hides my guilt.

I don't end it there,
So I grab my socks
And pull them straight down,
Until they are awk.

They sometimes get mad,
I mean them no harm.
They're just little pranks,
So I tell them mon.

I lead them forward
And out the front door.
I've charmed them with words,
Missaid evermore.

Noxon Road

There is a humble school
That sits just off a road
I think about her now
As I start to grow old.

I see her nestled there,
Noxon is her name,
You can spell it forward
And backwards just the same.

She taught me how to read
She taught me how to write
She taught me many things
I use each day and night.

I see me in her halls
I see me in her rooms
I see me on her swings
I see my friends costumed.

To her I give my thanks,
For when I was a child,
She shaped me as I am,
She loved me all the while.

My Sister

Once it seemed so scary
The feeling was so strange
Water half way up me,
From where came all this rain?

When my sister joined me,
My fear then went away.
She draws in red and blue,
She splashes and makes waves.

Sometimes she blows bubbles
And grabs them with her hands,
Pokes them with her fingers
And pops them when she can.

But what I love the most
Is sitting here with her,
Getting wet, in her arms,
Never saying a word.

Baby Bird

He holds me just right
Snuggled on his chest
All the world in sight
Like a bird in her nest.

I wish that I could fly,
Flap my arms like wings,
I would go so high
And see what soaring brings.

Right now this is fine,
Perched here on my dad.
They'll be time to fly,
I'm sure then he'll be sad.

So on and on I chirp,
Pausing here and there,
To mix in little burps,
Planting songs in the air.

Sassy's Shadow

Daddy and daughter
Out for a walk
The sun shines down
Silence is talk.

She sees dark
Where should be light
And pauses to think
On this funny sight.

What is that,
There on the ground?
Could it be me?
Where is my frown?

Almost a mirror
Short of reflection
Shadow's her name,
So what's the connection?

She follows me
Wherever I go
Is she my sister?
No, I think I know!

She looks up at Daddy
With her hand in his
And simply says "Sassy,"
For that's who it is.

And on we walk,
Our shadows in tow,
There to remind us
To take our days slow.

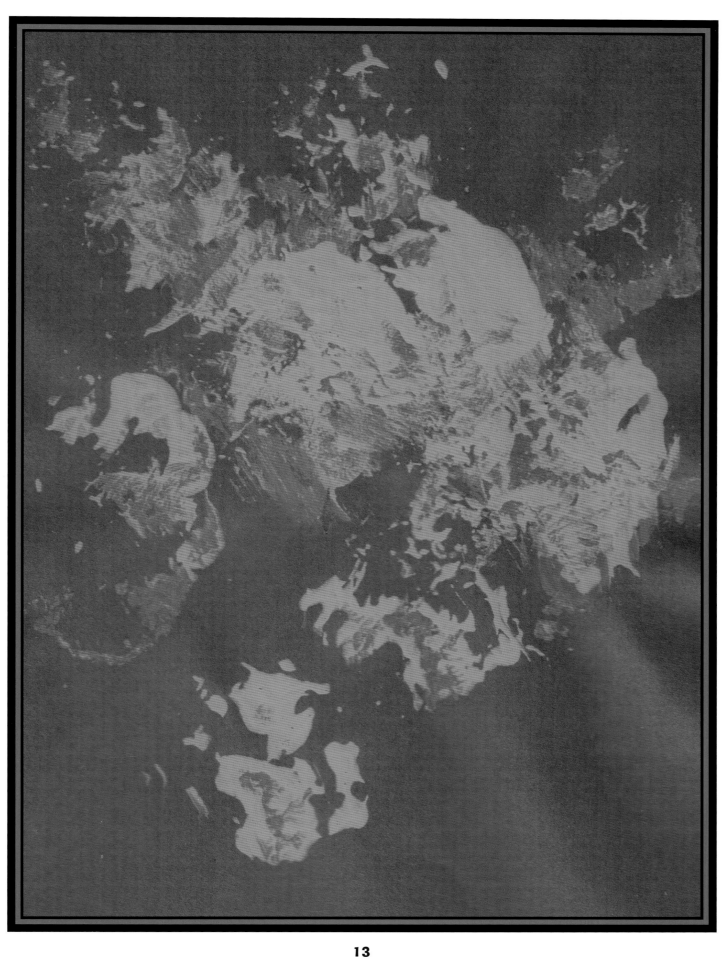

Little Rocks

They feel like little rocks
Growing in my mouth.
They look like small white blocks,
I wish that they'd come out!

I wake up in the dark,
Little rocks sure do hurt!
Why did all this start?
I'm drooling on my shirt!

They make me want to chew
I reach for any toy
Who cares if old or new
As long as it brings joy.

Right now this isn't fun
I cough to clear my throat
But soon the time will come
When dry shirts replace soaked.

Tying Our Shoes

Laces through sneakers
Laces through shoes
All tied in bows
Their curves hold the clues.

I sit on the stairs,
Momma sits down, too,
Then she weaves magic
Through my morning blues.

It seems so easy
Things Big people do,
Like brushing their teeth
And tying their shoes.

Left lace over right,
Then tuck under right,
The laces have crossed
Now, pull both ends tight.

That much I've learned
From Momma so far.
The first part's a cinch,
The ending is hard.

So, now here we go
To finish this task,
Momma's arms reach down,
Too fast these times pass.

Now, take your right thumb,
Forefinger, too,
Form loop between them,
Pinch, that's what you do.

With that half in place
We are almost done,
Pinch left lace the same,
Wrap over right thumb,

And over right loop,
Then under as well.
Give a push and pull,
Look! …Shhh, don't tell!

Of course ways differ
From girl to boy
With which side to start,
But that's not the point.

Don't see as boring
Such things that we do,
Like brushing our teeth
And tying our shoes.

We learn as we grow
But seem to forget
The joy in the new
Before the sun sets.

Finding Fun

It was a bitter winter's day,
Much too cold to go outside,
No snow added to boredom,
What could I do to have fun?

Upstairs,
Downstairs,

Nothing seemed to cross my mind.
Just then I looked at my bed,
My animals stared at me
And whispered in harmony.

They were real to me now,
No longer stuffed but with soul.
Not all were graced with a name,
But one was, the Bear of no brain.

Oddly, his voice was clearest,
Strange for my Bear of no brain.
All his friends followed his lead,
The word, though faint, was "read."

I took their advice up high
Where my books laid sloppily.
I stood on my stool and reached
And picked one from the shelf's heap.

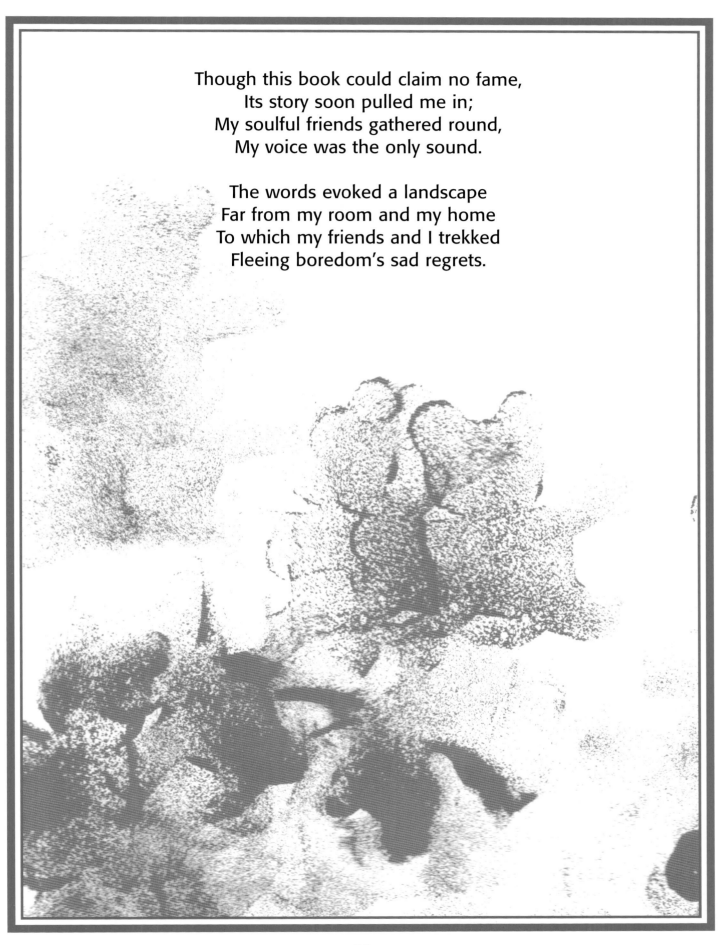

Though this book could claim no fame,
Its story soon pulled me in;
My soulful friends gathered round,
My voice was the only sound.

The words evoked a landscape
Far from my room and my home
To which my friends and I trekked
Fleeing boredom's sad regrets.

The Table

I pull myself up
When they turn their heads.
It's not very tough
As I hold the edge.

I now see the top,
Oh, what a mess!
A stander I'm not,
I lean in to rest.

I don't have much time
Before I must sit.
I'll grab what's not mine,
Then slowly I'll dip.

I'm back on the floor,
My prizes in hand.
I wish I had more,
I must learn to stand.

They say I will walk
Before I will crawl.
They sure like to talk,
I don't mind at all.

They don't even know,
I'm learning so quick.
My table stands low
And shares in my tricks.

Smiles While Sick

I am all smiles
Even when I'm sick
So say the grown ups
As I squirm and kick.

Five months I've been here
Five my nose has run
Maybe that's not true
Only my version.

Some days hearing hurts
As an ear has been plugged,
Others bring the rash,
Sore bottom and hugs.

My tummy's trouble
When I least expect
It empties on Dad
Mom cleans up the mess.

Fever is the worst,
For once I wake up
No one can get sleep,
Gone is the house hush.

Through all this turmoil,
Dad still lets me ride
High on his shoulders,
So, why should I cry?

I run my fingers
Through his graying hair.
My weary face glows,
For Dad's always there.

Her Life Runs Through Me

I find it just amazing
When daily I stop and think,
That she's no longer with us,
Yet still her spirit sings.

I hear her in my daddy
As he guides us through our lives;
His voice is kind and soothing
As he channels her with pride.

I look into my mirror
And see my rounded nose;
Old pictures soon reveal
A very kindred pose.

Perhaps that most cherished
Is when I say my name,
For lilies live forever,
Beyond the full moon's wane.

Although I never knew her,
Within me her life does flow;
This fact sustains me daily,
For loss is not my foe.

Peejays

Hand me down peejays
Giraffes and bumble bees
Stains from old sundaes
Wonderful, worn out knees.

Cozy, built-in slippers
Room for toes to wiggle
Rose buttons that glitter
Monkeys in the middle.

Fuzzy arms, fuzzy legs
Feathery fur gets stuck
Kitty rubs, kitty plays
Kissy kid plays tough.

Many night-nights have gone
Many more still to come
These peejays are warm
Could be the wet bottom.

Hand me down peejays
Grandpa hears me hiccup
Grandma sings away
Sleepies and sippie cups.

Bugs

Bugs abound in bed
Bugs are in my head
I shall not sleep then,
I'll stay up late again.

Mom and Dad show dismay
They've had a long day
They haven't any smiles
I'll make them stay awhile.

They won't watch the time
As I talk and I rhyme
Soon they'll laugh with me
In nighttime harmony.

Bugs abound in bed
So I've already said
They don't stop biting
Until I stop writing.

Author's Note to Parents

The title *Lilies on the Moon* derives from "Her Life Runs Through Me." The original title of this poem was "Her Blood Runs Through Us," but I thought the use of the word "blood" may scare some children. Changing "Us" to "Me" personalizes the poem.

My daughter, Cassidy Shoshana, has a passion for the moon and always seems to see it in the sky, even in the daytime when it is sometimes faintly visible. The name Shoshana is Hebrew for Lily. The lily is a bulbous, perennial flower. It comes back to life each year and most types produce a magnificent scent. The personal correlation is to my mother's name, Lillian, who died in 1974 when I was only six years old.

In addition to dedicating this book to her, I will be donating a portion of the profits from this book to facilities and organizations that are dedicated to children's health. I have personally witnessed the life-saving powers of a local hospital's Neonatal Intensive Care Unit (NICU).

I believe the health (physical, mental, emotional, etc.) and care of our children should be our main concern as adults who have witnessed a troubling world unfold in the last few years. My optimism is evident in the book's title: lilies can survive even on a waning moon, where no sign of life exists.

The watercolors, fingerpaints and down-right doodlings were created by Cassidy. She was born on Halloween in 2001. At first I thought I would make my own collages or perhaps use photographs. Then one day I looked closely at some of her creations.

The thought came to mind that if I were writing poetry for children that it naturally followed that a child should illustrate the book. If only my daughter Rachel Sarah were older (she was born July 26, 2003). She's a poet and artist in training, a crayon in one hand and a sippie cup in the other.

Common threads in the poems are conversation in silence, the innocence of childhood and the desire to somehow capture its magic forever. There are times when I do not need to verbalize thoughts to my daughters. Simply looking into their eyes, holding, hugging and the like speak volumes. I hope you enjoy the poems and the artwork with your family. Please stay in touch with us at www.kidzpoetz.com. May your life be blessed.

Carpe Diem
Robert W. Kurkela

Thanks

Dad and Marge for tolerating my whims and troubles over the years yet believing that somehow this writing venture would eventually materialize into something worthwhile. My brothers Craig, Walter, Scott and James for being influential on me in their own, unique ways. My nieces and my nephews for reminding me of why childhood is so sacred. My relatives no longer with me. June 8, 1979 8:02 PM. Robert Roeser for, among countless other things, our time writing poems together. GD. All my teachers in the Arlington Central School District. All my classmates from Arlington and SUNY Albany and those friends I've met since who find themselves now traveling through life. My daughters Cassidy and Rachel for redirecting my thoughts onto their everyday routines. My soulmate and wife, Lisa, for helping this book see the light of day and encouraging me with my words, although it often meant my disappearing into the basement for hours on end. To all who have been a part of my life so far and to those still to be met, I say "Thanks" for inspiring me.